After (H)ours

Ashwath Narayan

INDIA • SINGAPORE • MALAYSIA

ISBN 979-8-89233-543-0

Contents

Limerence & Murder

I saw a flash of something beautiful
Of this life being triumphful
I saw a version of me I wanted to be
A vision that's to never be

I had to consciously grieve
For the deaths I've had to see
Those people I saw in the sunset
Those people I never really met

The visions were but a glimmer
But they stayed on my mind on simmer
I couldn't focus on reality
My eyes fixated on the impossibility

I couldn't show up for myself
In present time when I needed
Because I was invested and seeded
Transfixed and already defeated

I was addicted to the limerence
In your absence my deliverance
But it too thrilled at hurting me
It was always going to end badly

I needed both feet back on the ground
It's pretty simple nothing profound
Murdered those people I had never seen
Cremated the dreams that had never been

Memories and ghosts are nice enough
But of my life to be the love of
It was you I chose
Now remain only the thorns of a withered rose

hurt feelings are just
momentary but love lasts
for eternity

Lover

I thought all my troubles would be over
Believed you really were my clover
No more wandering like a rover
I didn't expect this hangover
That the pain would carry over
My heart you did take over
My soul was yours to walk over
I was just a layover
Not permanent but a passover
I would have taken bullets for you my lover
I seek answers but your leaving *was* the closure
I'm left of melancholy a composer

all i want is to
dedicate my life to the
act of loving you

You're a Piece of Work

You're a piece of work, you know?
How much you've made me grow
I've been so frustrated and confused
Because I should be feeling used

But you go behaving your own way
Doing nice things and saving the day
What makes you think you have the right
To be the champion in my fight?

You're supposed to kick me down when I'm low
You're supposed to worsen the blow
Find ways to dim my glow
All these things you don't know

Who taught you to be like you?
To show me something new
The audacity to be so kind
And bring peace to my mind?

There's a way to behave
Push me in the direction of the grave
Instead you act in autonomy
Like you're the master of the sea

Compassion is against the rules
Yet you show it to even the fools
You have patience with the mules
Don't you know how to be cruel?

This kind of attitude is rash
You should be whipping a lash
Helping someone when they're down
Don't you know thorny is the crown?

You think just because you're so wise
That to imbeciles you can be nice
That you can wash the fires with your rain
And help alleviate a wretches pain?

This is not how things are done
Look at how the others have fun
They poke the creature with a stick
Each one takes their turn to kick

This display of righteousness
What brass callousness!
How dare you don't follow the crowd
This blasphemy who allowed?

How dare you change the theme?
Make a nightmare into a dream?
You better watch what you do
You might change destiny too

ultimately for
love there can always be a
clean slate and fresh start

My Love Will Sustain

If I am given the chance to love again
You will never have to explain
Or justify your pain
Nothing so inhumane
You will know you are sane
Alone you will never strain
If you're attacked I'll be a hurricane
On your enemies I will rain
Any one who hurts you slain
If I die I'll be born-again
I'll take the agonising pain
No matter the terrain
By your side I will remain
My love will sustain

You could have been my main
I would have taken your name
You dropped me like a game
From my pain what did you gain?
Love why did you feign?
I would have fought every campaign
Nothing would be able to tame
Nothing would be able to contain
Nothing could give you more fame
No love will ever be the same

i would have been fine
hoping for change that never
comes but by your side

Marry You

You were the love of my life
I thought I showed you
I thought in your heart you knew
How much I loved you

I thought you really knew
That I'd do anything for you
And that you loved me too
I hoped my dreams would come true

I believed I would marry you
To your greatest heights carry you
I thought you knew my love was true
How this kind of love is experienced by few

But I was expendable to you
You see yourself happier with someone new
Every day I have cried for you
On any day I would have died for you

But there's nothing I could ever do
You said I wasn't enough for you
Love was replaced by resentment and hate
Our time was over, my pleas too late

this house, like my heart,
is empty, grieving and
aching, it is haunted

Disbelief

I may be processing my grief
But I'm still in disbelief
I really need some relief
Of my heart you were a thief

I'm now empty except for pain
How did this havoc reign?
Nothing makes sense the same
I don't know if I'm even sane

It was not just my heart that shattered
Even my soul you left tattered
You were all that to me that mattered
But of my love you were never flattered

This wasn't even a remote possibility
This wasn't an alternate reality
It defied logic and rationality
But it is the world I now see

The same morning I dreamed of us
A beautiful marriage which wasn't a fuss
But all that became superfluous
You decided it was over, we didn't even discuss

i hope at least you
were aware that no one in
the world was more loved

You Can't Take My Memories

You can take your love away from me
Delete our pictures so no one will see
You can act like you don't remember loving me
But you can't take from me my memories

Grace

I wish I could have handled this with grace
I'm so embarrassed I must hide my face
I know this will leave a bad taste
I know I've lost myself the race

They say love has to be set free
I ask even if that means misery
If you love someone to that degree
Accept that he wants away from me

This is the most challenging task
That of me has ever been asked
I wish I had the strength to wear a mask
But for dishonesty I was miscast

I wish I could let you go
You don't want me anymore
How ever painful it may be
I can't force you to be with me

I had the best days that I've known
I have to let go the dreams that I'd sown
I have to realise the real thing
Imaginary was the ring

I have to back away
Accept you didn't want to stay
Hear the words that you say
Accept that that's the way

I got what so few do
Something that before I never knew
Love was real and I was happy too
Now I should be happy for you

I’m not the person whom you found
I’ve grown so much, it’s profound
Loving you lifted me off the ground
But to me you are not bound

i wish you could have
loved me until i learned how
to love myself too

Reflection

I don't spend time in front of the mirror
Don't look for my reflection in a river
My reflection in your eyes, I liked what I saw
You used to look at me like I was without flaw

does love mean nothing
when nothing is all that is
left when it is gone?

Another Start

A million times and more
I'd wait for you after you let me go
As many times as you break me
I'll wait hoping you wouldn't forsake me
Even though you broke my heart
I'll always be ready for another start

I wish you could have seen
Everything we could have been
I wish you could see
This current state is not permanency
That bad health is temporary
We could heal and be extraordinary

you were complete, you
were whole, you were enough, you
were everything

Shadow

You said this would be forever
But you abandoned me whenever
The slightest discomfort arose
A single thorn on our rose
Was too much to deal with
You didn't have the bandwidth
You'd declare it wasn't a fit
You didn't think I was worth it

But for you I'd take thorns and arrows
I'd persevere through times of sorrow
I'd fight so we have tomorrow
Any extra time together I'd borrow
I would stop a tornado
Destroy the status quo
I would never let you go
Fear I'd never let you know
To ego I'd never bow
Don't you remember our afterglow?

I'll always think of you as I go
Walking down any meadow
I'd conjure you a rainbow
We have magic, don't you know?
The fields I will plough
Dreams I will sow
Just to be your shadow

I thought you were my prize
For 30 years of honest tries
30 years of desperate cries
A lifetime without highs
For telling no lies
I couldn't believe my eyes

Of dark days I thought this meant the end
Forever you'd be my friend
At the rapture together we'd ascend
On each other we could always depend
You would never lie or pretend
Our love, you too, would defend

forever can last
a lifetime or be over
before you know it

Stand in the Sun

I could take on any pain
All the pain
Every burden, challenge I'd entertain
Earthquake, tornado, hurricane
Everyday could be the same
But I'd take it all and more
I'd take it all no matter how sore
Because I had already won
Nothing could make me come undone
Back when you and I were one
I could stand in the sun

The Tax Man Cometh

This feels like borrowed time
I've outlived the life that was mine
And now the universe has lost its patience
Vengeance has replaced its earlier complaisance
It's clear its no longer messing about
The universe won't stop till I'm out

The circumstances couldn't be worse
Not even by a witch's curse
This reality is tragically perverse
So many wounds to nurse
So much I have to reimburse
Ain't no *Tax Man* like the universe

I Wanted

I wanted you to think I was strong
That I tried my best to do no wrong
I wanted you to think I was brave
That I fought the demon to stay out of a grave

I hoped you would think I was a survivor
Fearless like a skydiver
Someone who should be angry and destructive
But despite the odds is reconstructive

I hoped you would think I had integrity
That I was better than I thought I ought to be
I wished you would see my personality
The real one beneath the one temporary

I hoped you saw that I loved with a passion
That for you I'd always have compassion
You'd never have to fear you'd be alone
With me you would always have a home

I'll Wait

This wasn't chance, it was by design
It is written in our bloodline
My heart to you I consign
Love we can redefine
My will is mighty like the river Rhein

I'll wait on the sideline
Till time for me you assign
Till we are connected and back online
I'll wait till we walk the shoreline
I'll wait till we dance under the moonshine
I'll wait till on your face I see the sunshine
I'll wait till every night together we dine
I'll wait till our lives again entwine
I'll wait till we're aged like fine wine

I’ll wait till you see a sign
I’ll wait till the stars align
I’ll wait till the end of time
I’ll wait till once again you are mine

Outshine

When we converge our lifeline
The universe we can redesign
When our souls we realign
There will be fireworks on the skyline
When our light we combine
Even the sun we will outshine

every dream of mine
came true; i found love and a
family in you

Touch Your Face

Even if the stars interface
Like a memory you'll only be a trace
I wont get to touch your face
I won't get the warmth of your embrace
My world is empty like outer space

Just In Case

I keep trying just in case
I manage to showcase
A love you're willing to retrace
One I hope you didn't already replace

Happiness With Someone New

I have to let go
If peace I ever want to know
For new dreams to sow
To learn from this and grow

But I don't want to let you go
The depths of my love you never knew
This much love is deserved by few
In absence of any conditionality too

I would rather exist in this pain
And about what we lost complain
Because I'd rather have pain with you
Than happiness with someone new

Eclipse

It's just for a brief moment
But for that brief moment
The moon blocks out the entire sun
The entire fucking sun
Incredible
Our love is like an eclipse
Rare
Spectacular
Over too soon
I am the moon

you are the wisdom
of experience and the
brightest light of youth

Still Standing

This is a challenge. My toughest challenge.
But it's a challenge. Just another.
I've faced so many. Made it this far.
Still standing.

I may fall. But I get back up.
I'm stubborn. I'm strength.
I'm resilience. I'm perseverance.
I can overcome this.
I can get over you.
I don't want to.

Go forth my lover,
Go forth and find another.
In another life
I hope we find each other
I'll wait for you forever

Babylon

When the heart stops beating
And the soul begins retreating
The sun sets for its final time
For you are no longer mine

How does life go on
When we no longer liaison?
We are the rubble of Babylon
Something beautiful that's gone

would you call me a
liar if i told you that
the world was on fire?

Hello, Darkness

No one will ever sing along
They don't know the words of the song
That's for the best, it's not wrong
Alone, I must be headstrong

To give in to the darkness is tempting
For the darkness says with me she can sing
That she'll take me under her wing
That peace and relief only she can bring

The problem has not be the dark night
It's that I've been living under the light
Bad things happened because I was in sight
She says this and it sounds right

This energy that I attract
That follows me no matter how I act
I look for logic, I look for fact
It must be because I'm not intact

In me there is something familiar
The darkness recognises the colour
Perhaps it seeps even out of my ear
And that's why it's always near

It asks me to embrace it, not to fear
It will remove the fog, makes things clear
It sounds so honest, so sincere
It even wipes away my tears

It tells me to accept the truth
Accept it while I still have youth
Its voice is velvet like vermouth
The journey to hell will be smooth

When I am birthed from a poisonous tree
Of course there will be poison in me
It's obvious, it's not hard to see
Of darkness how could I be free?

All the inner conflict will end
If I no longer tried to pretend
The darkness will be my friend
The light never turns up to defend

The darkness reminds me
I was abandoned even by family
The one I love doesn't love me
In my absence he'll still be happy

The darkness urges me to come along
I don't need to fear as it is strong
It will even sing with me a swan song
To reject my only offer of help would be wrong

The darkness offers me a chalice
A liquid filled with black and malice
I could be living in a palace
See stars and the aurora borealis

It makes an offer that's hard to resist
From my lover I'll never again be kissed
When I'm gone I won't be missed
It asks to form a pact, a tryst

It's a tempting offer, don't you agree?
Would you accept it if you were me?
But alas! For today, I choose the misery
Today that darkness won't have me

In my heart of hearts there is a light
So strong it fends off the darks might
A rider on an immortal horse, a knight
The hope my love returns to me one night

Agony

For a few moments each morning
I'm not in agony
While my bones ache
My mind is at ease
The dogs are hungry
And demand to be fed
It's only once they've started eating
And I've sat down with my coffee
That reality sets in
You haven't come down the stairs
You aren't going to come down
You aren't here
Then, comes the agony

Prisoner of War

I wake up feeling hungover
Like I've travelled and had a long layover
Like I've been a pushover
It didn't take a hostile takeover
I'm a prisoner of war, a leftover

grief is infinite
it rears its unwelcome head
at the dead of night

Today & Everyday

How could you walk away
When you know I know no other way
That for you here I'd stay
Today and everyday

Morning Dew

Everything reminds me of you
The morning dew
Things old and new
Things several or few
Every colour, every hue
No matter what I do
I find myself thinking of you

The Ocean

We are the ocean, you and I
A horizon as far as can be seen by the eye
The calm, deep waters are you
You make me every shade of blue

The Graveyard of My Mind

Am I to bury you now
In the graveyard of my mind?
The graveyard of my mind
It's a place unkind
It's where demons I bind
It's where pain I find
It's all I left behind

Chance

We never got the chance
For a lovely night of romance
A night just to dance
A night to be in a trance
To in bliss to prance
For our love to grow in expanse
For us to advance
Now you've taken a stance
If only we had a chance

Collateral Damage

Not enough credit is given
To those that are the bystanders
The significant others
Sometimes the fiercest supporters
Sometimes collateral damage
But they're there, or were
Confused, and blindfolded
Because they can't see the demons
They only hear you screaming
It's got to be hard, to say the least
Helping to fight an invisible beast
The cursed are tormented, no doubt
But their consorts and friends
They aren't entirely spared
They maybe scared
They maybe scarred

Sometimes your vision is theirs
And with your seeing eyes they understand
They see you fall and help you stand
But sometimes they see through you
Where there's only dust and shadow
It's not a fault or shortcoming
It's just one of those things
They see you hide from the world
But to them it's a safe place
They don't need to hide in your bunker
Your way of existence doesn't satiate their hunger
And release them to the world you must
They can spread their wings in the light
They don't need to quiver in fright
They should live, truly live
For life is fragile and fleeting
They may not have stayed forever
But they stayed a while
Even though they didn't see the demons
Even though you *had* demons

They stayed a while
And the demons didn't entirely spare them
There was no need for them to feel pain too
You had enough pain for both of you
He left
And that was devastating
But he did stay all those days
And he was your sun's rays
He gave you more than anyone else
Cherish that, celebrate that
And celebrate that he is free
Free to live the life he chooses
Unbound, unchained, demon-free
Maybe live through him vicariously
But let him be
What and where he wants to be
And if you did right by him
He'll know you didn't take him for granted
That you know that it wasn't easy for him
That you know he tried

But trying to love is exhausting
It's not how it should be
But he tried, despite the demons
Fuck, voluntarily tried, *with* DEMONS
He's probably as insane as you are
And so he needs the stability you can't give him
Maybe one day he'll realise who you are
Separate the demons from the human
And he'll then be able to remember you fondly
And he'll be your shared historian
Of a time that was beautiful
Of dreams that were fantastical
And he'll smile from his heart
But until then, you can remember still
He changed your life, and you
And in doing that he was robbed
Of his vision of the world
One where demons don't exist
And where hope isn't an idea but a noun
It's not a small sacrifice

Knowing the truth of world comes with a price
He paid it, now forever burdened with the truth
Of knowing demons exist, just to him unseen
He doesn't need to be collateral damage
When he finds the love that he wants
He should know that his happiness is yours
But your pain doesn't need to be his
Bittersweet things, are at least in part, sweet.

Exodus

If this is not an exodus
I don't what is
Who will lead me into *The Promised Land*?

Escaped from Pandora's Box

I always said there was something nefarious about
hope
How it tortured those who are cursed to cope
It is a cruel hoax
Like all evil it came from Pandora's Box

The Conductor

The conductor
Of the bus
Of the orchestra
Of my heart
Is there a bus
That will take me back to the start?

You Own My Heart

The sun owns the flowers
That bloom in its light
That bask in its warmth
And fight even gravity
For a chance to see its master's face

The moon owns the ocean
And draws up the water
That form the mighty waves
From the beginning of time to the end of days

The stars are owned by the sky
Their blazing fires up high
Drawing constellations in their wake
The art of the heavens are their make

And it is you
You who owns my heart
You did from the start
You did when we part

Unstoppable Force

You were the immovable object
I thought I was the unstoppable force
I wasn't

Encore

It's been several months now and more
I still hope it's you at the door
Back for an encore
Thirsting for more
It won't be like before
This time you're sure

Noah's Arc

I was shovelling out bucket after bucket
Of the water that was filling up the boat
Trying to the plug the hole with my body
Desperate to keep afloat, keep us alive
It mattered not to you that we were sinking
You had long before planned to disembark
We were counterparts on Noah's arc
Now I'm paddling alone in the dark

Before You Walked Out the Door

You moved on a long time ago
Long before you walked out the door
You're happy and I'm glad you are
Your pictures show you've travelled far

I'm still on the floor where you left me
Hoping all these months you'd come back for me
Because we said our love was forever
We were always going to be together
I was yours and you my lover
We could recover, rediscover love

You pretend like I never existed
That your love was never real to be trusted
That I shouldn't stop the ship from going down
Now I'm lost never again to be found

Who Knows Me Better Than You?

I know I'm broken, I know I'm scarred
I know being with me is hard
I wish you saw the soldier in me
Fighting demons so with you I could be
This dark night is but temporary

Don't you see what I've survived?
To fight this war who else would have even tried?
Don't you see the light inside me?
Under the dark shroud it hides in me
A light unmatched in love and glory

I wanted to give you the world and more
To make you happy like you've never been before
To be your companion through space and time
Give you everything including the life that's mine
Unconditional, unwavering, a love divine

These demons I could had defeated
A healthy mind I could have created
Your existence I would have venerated
For the love in me that you generated
Is power, magic, beauty to be celebrated

But my unhealed wounds made me flammable
My feelings beyond controllable
Accountability was to my perception and the past
To old wounds that forever wouldn't last
I wish you had heard me before I was outcast

You were not attacked, you weren't blamed
I took all the blame to my name
But by then your perception of me was black
You were repulsed by me, my mere presence an attack
I could say nothing to love bring back

Don't you see this undying love in me?
That no matter what I'll never at you be angry
Did you not feel my loyalty, devotion and sincerity?
The stars in my eyes when you I see?
That I'd do anything to make you happy?

You have seen the depths of me
Every dream, every demon, every insecurity
But even you doubted my intentions of purity
How could it then ever be a possibility
To have faith in anyone to really see me?

You saw me as the demon with which I fight
You saw me as a demon who wished to steal your light
You alone know me in entirety
You concluded I wasn't unlike the evil who sired me
Perhaps then it is true, for I showed you all of me

scapegoat, silent lamb,
black sheep; does the lion lose sleep
over all that's me?

Stories

You came into my life like a dream
In you I found love and my team
You were my friend, lover and teacher
Shed light on my false portrayal of a preacher

I learned the true magic of love
That the real power is not in being loved
But in loving, it's about the other not the self
I don't have pictures of myself on a shelf

I learned to open my heart
I learned about the wonder of art
I learned to see the good and the light
I learned I was stronger than evil's might

I had to lose you to find myself
My inner soldier, champion and bookshelf
I have so many books and stories inside me
So much that I'm sorry you didn't see

But I'm learning that that's okay
That perhaps my waters were much too deep
I wouldn't have wanted you to drown
I'm happy to see you still wear your crown

I'm sad that you were too distracted to see
So you would at be able to look back
With fondness and serenity
Because you had magic when you had me

you were my island
of stability in this
world that is but chaos

Fact

That my heart was broken is just a fact
It's not a loaded statement or attack
It's not to induce guilt or manipulate
I wish it didn't promote more hate

Leaving me was not a crime
It's not wrong to want to not waste time
To want better for oneself is good
Have that desire everyone would

You have the autonomy for your actions
No obligation to my reaction
You can my love return with hate
In love and life nothing is fair or obligate

Our experiences both together and apart
Were not the same right from the start
You've seen the world, marvellous art
I only know what's in my heart

Just because my love is true
Doesn't make me entitled to you
I may see treasure but you see trash
I may walk through fire but your desire may not be ash

Although I feel hurt and betrayed
And wish we better parlayed
There's nothing you could do
That I wouldn't have been willing to work through

Two things can be simultaneously true
In heartbreak and devastation I can still love you
Your happiness is what I want most
I'll be happy with our memories, and your ghost

will it be a while
till our differences we
truly reconcile?

Entitled

I wanted so badly to hear aloud
That of me you were proud
I wished you could think of me
As a person with whom you wanted to be

I wished you saw me as special
Saw in me love and potential
I was a soldier and champion this year
I hoped you'd think me enough to keep near

I was too emotional to be thought smart
I tried to keep you interested with art
I cooked, baked, painted from my heart
If I didn't earn your presence I feared you'd depart

I knew that I needed time
To fix all the broken parts that were mine
Defeat the demons in my mind
Then could give you a love nowhere else you'd find

How could I have been so entitled to believe
I could ask for you not to leave
When at the time when you did depart
All I could offer you was my broken parts

I thought I had the right to fight
For the love I knew was right
Because I thought you had felt it too
That we belonged together, me and you

I thought you felt what I had
The belief then would have thought you mad
To not do everything possible to save the love
There was no other option, orders from above

I wish you could have seen through my eyes
Not the vision of demons that make me cry
But the wonder that you are in my perception
You are crafted in light and beauty, perfection

I wish you knew that I was in awe of you
Of your calm composure and strong mind
Your confidence and charisma made you glow
That such beauty could exist I didn't ever know

I wish you knew that my only dream
Was to give you the world, make you happy
To make you feel safe and secure
My intentions I promise were pure

I wish you could know I adored you
That I saw the world and more in you
I wish the depths of my love you knew
I wish that you knew my love was true

In you I found a heart I could trust
And it was only with you that I ever discussed
All my vulnerability, pain and shame
All my fears I told you by name

I thought that you would believe
That while I was broken quite harrowingly
I was not like the evil that defiled me
And my love for you couldn't be matched by any

The only person in the entire universe
And likely no other will I ever so immerse
Knowing all of me, the darkness too
There won't be another like you

I cared for the opinion of not another soul
Didn't care what I was thought of by the world, the whole
That validation by you in being seen and believed
Was all I wanted or would ever need

love is forever
learning, forever growing
love is unlimited

We Could Have Fixed It

I wish I had given you reason to stay
I wish I hadn't let things come in the way
I wish everything of my life before me met
Disappeared and not even memory I had kept
I wish I was able to communicate right
How badly I failed, it always led to a fight
How am I supposed to get over you
When I know this love was true
And we could have fixed it like it was new

ultimately at
the end neither i nor love
proved to be enough

What is Right?

I know you said you wanted out
And I understand your words I have no doubt
And I respect you so I want to conform
To the boundaries you set, the new reform
And I know I said I will let you be in peace
From me and my darkness you'd have release
And I understand because you don't share
My feelings and how much for you I care
That my persistence and lingering attachment
Are an annoyance and you're in disenchantment

But damn, it's hard
I'm constantly on guard
For the urge to reach out to you is strong
For my heart thinks it's with you that I belong
Even now it sings your song
Hoping against hope you'll sing along
And because I want to fight
For a love that I know is right
It's with myself that I now have to fight
To control myself, do what is right
But what is right?

what madness is this
spending fleeting time apart
when you have my heart?

Some Days

Some days I feel wise
Some days I'm a fool in disguise
So many lessons learned
So many times burned
So many mistakes made in the past
Still making mistakes since I checked last

opposing facts can
simultaneously
coexist in truth

Magic

Everyday I think about you
Everyday I think of you and smile
Loving you was the greatest joy of my life
Loving you was the beginning of possibility
The possibility of incredible things
The possibility that pulled heart-strings
You aren't here but my days aren't grey
You aren't here but I'm doing okay
I'm doing okay
I'm growing and evolving and living
I'm changing and improving
I'm learning to love everything you couldn't
I'm learning to love all of me
I'm learning about the world and wonder
I'm learning about *magic*
I'm learning about *me*

I see bravery in my admission of fear
I see endearment in wishing you were near
I see wisdom in every fallen tear
I can tell myself what I wanted from you to hear
I'm finding in myself everything I need
I'm finding in myself safety
I'm finding in myself love
I'm finding in myself a home
I'm still finding these things in me
I'm not looking for you anymore
But I had found those things in you
Now I'm finding myself anew

www.ingramcontent.com/pod-product-compliance
Lightning Source LLC
LaVergne TN
LVHW091048150826
845673LV00002B/504

9798892335430